A New True Book

URANUS

By Dennis B. Fradin

CHILDRENS PRESS®
CHICAGO

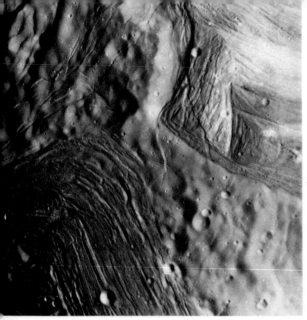

PHOTO CREDITS
AP/Wide World Photos—37
Art—John Forsberg—8-9
The Bettmann Archive—21, 22, 29
Finley Holiday Film Corporation—13
Historical Pictures Service, Chicago—19
Art—Len Meents—32
NASA—2, 6, 12 (center), 31
NASA-JET PROPULSION LAB—Cover, 11 (2 photos), 12 (top), 39, 41, 42, 43
National Optical Astronomy Observatories—18
North Wind Picture Archives—15
Chart courtesy Odyssey Magazine—10
Photri—4, 12 (bottom), 17, 24, 26, 33 (2 photos), 34 (2 photos), 45
Cover—Painting shows *Voyager II* passing Uranus on its journey toward Neptune.

Voyager II photographed the surface of Miranda, a moon orbiting Uranus.

Library of Congress Cataloging-in-Publication Data

Fradin, Dennis B.
Uranus / by Dennis B. Fradin

p.   cm. — (A new true book)
Includes index.
Summary: Discusses the seventh planet, how it was named, and the information astronomers have gathered about it.
ISBN 0-516-01177-4
1. Uranus (Planet)—Juvenile literature. [1. Uranus (Planet)] I. Title.
QB681.F73 1989   89-9984
523.4'7—dc20   CIP
                                   AC

TABLE OF CONTENTS

Stars...5

Planets...7

The Five Planets of the
    Ancients...11

Copernicus Learns the Truth...15

Uranus Is Discovered...19

Naming the New Planet...27

Uranus Points the Way to Neptune
    and Pluto...30

What Telescopes Revealed...33

What *Voyager II* Revealed...38

More Questions About Uranus...44

Words You Should Know...46

Index...47

STARS

There are millions of stars in space. We can see several thousand stars at night with just our eyes. Telescopes reveal millions more.

All the stars but one can be seen only at night. The one daytime star is the Sun. Light from the Sun gives us our daytime.

The Sun and all the other stars are giant balls

The Sun is a star.

of hot glowing gas. They shine by their own light. The stars seem to twinkle, or blink, at night. This happens because our Earth's air plays tricks with the starlight.

PLANETS

Planets are large objects that orbit (move around) stars. Probably millions of stars have planets. But all the stars except one are too far away for us to see their planets in detail. The Sun is the only star whose planets we have studied closely.

The Sun has nine known planets. Hot Mercury is the nearest planet to the Sun.

Then come Venus, Earth,
Mars, Jupiter, and Saturn.
Uranus comes seventh.
Neptune is eighth, and
frozen Pluto is ninth.

There are three ways to
spot planets. First, planets
don't twinkle. The reason
is that planets don't shine
by their own light. They

only reflect the sunlight.
Our air plays less tricks
with reflected light than it
does with starlight.

Second, planets appear
to move differently from
stars. They seem to move
among the stars over time.
This happens because the
planets are orbiting the Sun.

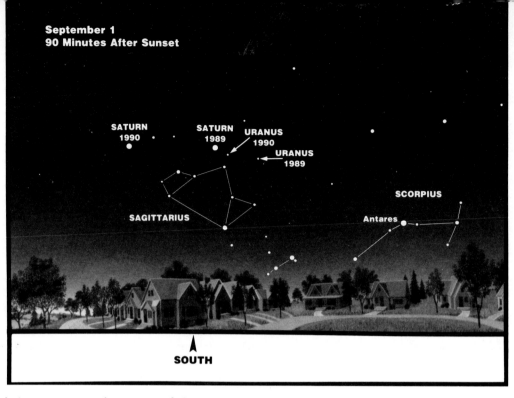

SATURN
1990

SATURN
1989

URANUS
1990

URANUS
1989

SCORPIUS

SAGITTARIUS

Antares

SOUTH

Astronomers make maps of the stars in the sky.

There is a third way to find the planets. You can get a special sky map. Astronomy magazines have them. These maps show where to spot the planets at any given time.

THE FIVE PLANETS OF THE ANCIENTS

Ancient people thought there were just five planets—Mercury, Venus, Mars, Jupiter, and Saturn. All five are bright enough to be seen with just our eyes.

On about thirty-five days a year, Mercury can be seen near sunset or sunrise. The

Mariner X photographs of Mercury (left) and Venus (right)

Mars

Saturn

Jupiter

white planet Venus is the brightest object in the sky besides the Sun and the Moon. Mars is bright and red. Jupiter is bright and yellow-white. Saturn is not quite as bright as Jupiter and is a bit more yellowish.

At times Uranus can barely be seen with just

the eye if you know where to look and if you are in a very dark place. But the ancients did not spot Uranus. And they never saw Neptune and Pluto. It takes a telescope to see those two planets.

What about our home planet, Earth? Anyone can

Earth

see our Earth just by looking down at the ground. The ancients saw Earth, of course, but they didn't know that it was a planet. They thought that Earth was a special object at the center of space. They thought that all the planets and even the stars circled Earth. They did not know that Earth and the other planets orbit the Sun. And they did not know that the other stars don't come anywhere near Earth.

COPERNICUS LEARNS THE TRUTH

Nicolaus Copernicus
(1473-1543)

The idea that the planets and stars orbit Earth lasted until about 500 years ago. The main discoverer of the truth was the Polish astronomer Nicolaus Copernicus.

15

Copernicus showed that
the Sun is just one among
many millions of stars. He
proved that the planets
orbit the Sun. The Sun and
its planets are the main
members of what became
known as the Solar
System. The Solar System
can be thought of as the
Sun's "family" of objects.

Moons are part of the
Solar System, too. Moons
are objects that orbit most

COMET

PLUTO

NEPTUNE

URANUS

SUN
SPOTS

SATURN

ASTEROIDS

MERCURY

VENUS

MARS

EARTH

MOON

JUPITER

Our Solar
System is
made up of
planets, moons,
asteroids,
and comets.

of the planets. Comets are
also part of the Solar
System. They travel in long
orbits around the Sun.
Comets are made of ice,
gas, and dust. They have
long, glowing tails when
they are near the Sun.

This comet, IRAS-Araki-Alcock, was photographed on May 8, 1983. The head of the comet is at the lower left.

Sometimes comets can be seen from Earth.

Copernicus lived before people had telescopes. So he thought there were just six planets—Mercury, Venus, Earth, Mars, Jupiter, and Saturn.

18

URANUS IS DISCOVERED

Galileo (1564-1642)
with his telescope

The telescope was invented in about 1608. Galileo of Italy was the first famous astronomer to use a telescope. Galileo made many discoveries. He learned that the Milky Way is made of millions of

19

stars. He learned that Jupiter has moons. But he did not find Uranus. Uranus wasn't discovered until William Herschel spotted the planet in 1781.

William Herschel was born in Hannover, Germany. He moved to England around the age of twenty. He earned his living by playing the organ and teaching music. But at about the age of thirty-five, he took up astronomy as a

William Herschel, the discoverer of Uranus, lived from 1738 to 1822. He studied the stars with his sister, Caroline.

hobby. He built telescopes and made great discoveries with them. His sister, Caroline Herschel, worked with him and made some discoveries of her own.

Herschel's
forty-foot
reflecting
telescope

On the night of March 13, 1781, Herschel was looking for double stars near the border of the constellations Taurus the Bull and Gemini the Twins. He saw an unknown greenish object in this region.

Herschel knew it wasn't
a star. It didn't twinkle.
Also, stars are so distant
from Earth that they look
like points of light even in
a telescope. This object
looked like a little ball.
That is how planets look.
Comets also look like little
balls when far from the
Sun.

At first Herschel thought
he had found a comet. He
wrote papers and letters
about it. This helped other
astronomers find the

Voyager II
photograph of
Uranus, taken
from 1.7 million
miles away
from the planet

object. Herschel studied
his object many more
times during the next
months. Finally, all the
astronomers agreed.
William Herschel had
discovered planet number
seven! It was the first

discovery of a planet since ancient people had first seen Mercury, Venus, Mars, Jupiter, and Saturn.

Astronomers studied old records. They found that the seventh planet had been seen in telescopes more than twenty times before William Herschel's discovery! The first such sighting had been made back in 1690 by John Flamsteed of England. But Flamsteed and the others

Voyager II was 600,000 miles away when it took this photograph of Uranus.

who had seen the seventh planet hadn't known what it was. Herschel was the first to show that it was a planet. That is why we say that Herschel and not Flamsteed discovered Uranus.

NAMING
THE NEW PLANET

At first many people called the new object "Herschel's Planet" or "Herschel." Some people hoped that one of these names would become its official name. One of the many other suggested names was "Dumbbell." Why this strange name? The planet had made dumbbells of astronomers by going undiscovered for so long!

Herschel himself wanted to call it "Georgium Sidus" (George's Star) to honor England's King George III. But many people opposed this name. First, the object was a planet, not a star. Second, many people disliked King George III. When Herschel made his discovery, the American colonies were fighting to break free of George III and English rule.

The other planets had been named for ancient

Like many of the other objects in our Solar System, Uranus was named after an ancient god.

gods and goddesses. Many people thought that the new planet should be, too. Johann E. Bode of Germany liked the name Uranus. It was the name of the Greek and Roman god of the sky. Uranus won out as the name of the new planet.

URANUS POINTS THE WAY TO NEPTUNE AND PLUTO

Gravity is the force that holds objects together in space. The Sun's gravity keeps Earth from flying off into space. Earth's gravity keeps the Moon from flying off, and holds us to the ground.

Astronomers soon saw something strange about Uranus. Sometimes it wobbled away from the

Sun. The gravity of something to the outside seemed to be pulling at Uranus. Astronomers thought this something might be an eighth planet. They searched the sky. In 1846 the eighth planet was discovered. It was named Neptune.

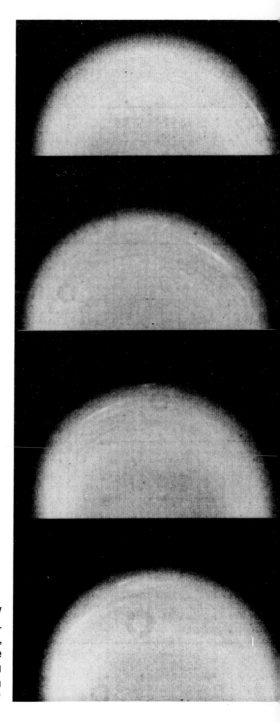

Time-lapse photographs show changing features on Uranus. Do you see the two small, bright, streaky clouds on the top photograph? Can you see how they have moved on the bottom photograph?

Something seemed to be tugging at Neptune from the outside, too. Also, something in addition to Neptune still seemed to be tugging at Uranus. Astronomers searched for a ninth planet. It was found in 1930 and named Pluto.

MERCURY

VENUS

EARTH

MARS

JUPITER

SATURN

URANUS

NEPTUNE

PLUTO

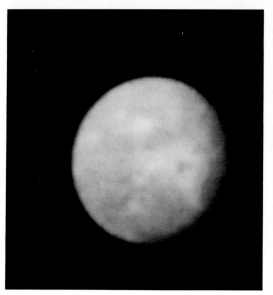

Oberon (left) and Miranda (right) are moons of Uranus.

WHAT TELESCOPES REVEALED

Telescopes helped astronomers learn a lot about Uranus in the 200 years after its discovery. In 1787 William Herschel discovered two moons of

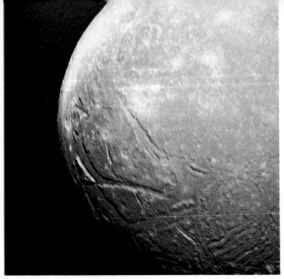

Voyager photographed Titania (left) and Ariel (right), moons of Uranus

Uranus. Two more were found in 1851. Uranus's fifth moon was found in 1948.

Telescopes also showed that Uranus is very big. Of the nine planets, only Jupiter and Saturn are bigger than Uranus. Our Earth could fit inside Uranus over 60 times!

Astronomers found that when we view Uranus, we are not seeing its surface. We are seeing clouds over the planet. These clouds are made of gases that would be poisonous to us. Belts can be seen on the clouds. They do not stretch across the planet from side to side like Jupiter's belts. They go up and down. This is because Uranus is lying on its side as it rotates, or spins.

Astronomers learned that,

in places, the temperature in Uranus's clouds is colder than -300° F. Uranus's atmosphere is so cold because the planet is so far from the Sun. Uranus takes eighty-four years to orbit the Sun because of its great distance. This means that Uranus's year is eighty-four earth-years long.

In 1977 astronomers learned something new about Uranus. Saturn had been thought to be the

Uranus was discovered to have rings around it just like Saturn.

only planet with rings.
Uranus was found to have
rings, too. Jupiter was also
found to have a ring about
that time.

WHAT VOYAGER II REVEALED

No telescope on Earth can provide a clear picture of Uranus. The planet is too far away. During the mid-1900s, scientists found a way to see the planets up close. They began launching space probes toward the planets. Space probes carry no people. They carry instruments that send photos and data back to Earth.

Painting shows *Voyager II* passing by Uranus on its journey toward Neptune.

In 1977 the United States launched the *Voyager I* and *Voyager II* space probes. The Voyager mission was to study Jupiter, Saturn,

Uranus, and Neptune.

The Voyager probes provided a great deal of new data about Jupiter in 1979. They revealed much about Saturn in 1980-1981. *Voyager II* then went on to Uranus, and passed near the planet in early 1986. The probe provided a wealth of data about Uranus and its moons.

Astronomers had not known how long Uranus takes to spin one time.

A view of Uranus and its rings as seen from Miranda

Voyager II learned that Uranus spins once in about 17¼ hours. This means that a day on Uranus is about 17¼ hours long.

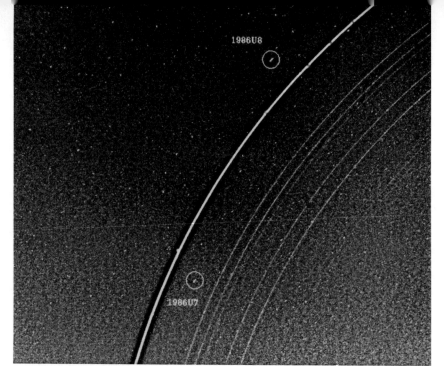

Uranus has nine rings. Scientists have photographed two of its moons, 1986U8 and 1986U7.

Voyager II found ten new little moons of Uranus. This brought Uranus's total to fifteen. Only Saturn and Jupiter have more moons. *Voyager II* also obtained great views of Uranus's five biggest moons.

The rings of Uranus are full of moving dust particles, which appear as bright streaks on this photograph.

   Uranus's rings were found to be made of large chunks of rock and ice. And it was found that Uranus seems to have a very hot ocean beneath its cold clouds.

MORE QUESTIONS ABOUT URANUS

Scientists still have many questions about Uranus. Why is the seventh planet tipped over on its side? Did something slam into Uranus and knock it over? Does Uranus really have a very hot ocean? If so, is it made of melted comets that Uranus swept up? What formed the rings?

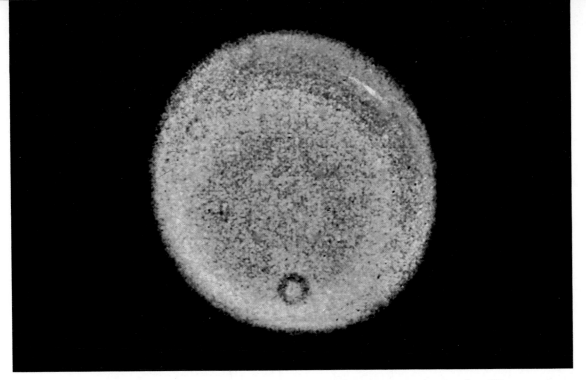

In many ways Uranus is still a mystery.

Could there be any life on
Uranus?

Someday more probes
will be sent to Uranus. They
will help us learn more about
the distant planet that
William Herschel discovered
more than 200 years ago.

FACTS ABOUT URANUS

Average Distance from Sun— About 1,780,000,000 (one billion, 780 million) miles

Closest Approach to Earth— About 1,700,000,000 (one billion, 700 million) miles

Diameter—About 32,000 miles

Length of Day—About 17¼ hours

Length of Year—About 84 earth-years

Temperatures—Places in Uranus's clouds are colder than -300° F; but below the clouds Uranus may have a very hot ocean

Atmosphere—Mainly hydrogen, helium, methane

Number of Moons—At least 15

Weight of an Object on Uranus That Would Weigh 100 Pounds on Earth—93 pounds

Average Speed as Uranus Orbits the Sun—About 4 miles per second

WORDS YOU SHOULD KNOW

ancient(AIN • shent)—very old

astronomer(ast • RAH • nih • mer)—a person who studies stars, planets, and other heavenly bodies

atmosphere(AT • muss • feer)—the gases surrounding some heavenly bodies

billion(BILL • yun)—a thousand million (1,000,000,000)

comet(CAHM • it)—an object (made of ice, gas, and dust) that has a long, glowing tail when near the Sun

constellation(kahn • stel • LAY • shun)—a star group in a certain area of the sky

double star(DUB • il STAHR)—two stars that are very close together or that only look like they are very close together

Earth(ERTH)—the planet (the third from the Sun) on which we live

gravity(GRAV • ih • tee)—the force that holds things down to a heavenly body

heavenly body(HEV • en • lee BAHD • ee) — an object in space,
  such as a star, planet, or moon

hobby(HAH • bee) — something a person does for fun

million(mil • yun) — a thousand thousand (1,000,000)

moon(MOON) — a natural object that orbits a planet; Uranus has at
  least 15 moons

orbit(OR • bit) — the path an object takes when it moves around
  another object

planet(PLAN • it) — a large object that orbits a star; the Sun has
  nine planets

reflect(ree • FLEKT) — to throw back

Solar System(SOH • ler SISS • tim) — the Sun and its "family" of
  objects

space probe(SPAISS PROHB) — an unmanned spacecraft sent
  to study heavenly bodies

star(STAHR) — a giant ball of hot, glowing gases

Sun(SUHN) — the yellow star that is the closest star to Earth

telescope(TEL • ih • skohp) — an instrument that makes distant
  objects look closer

Uranus(YOO • rih • nuss) — the seventh planet from the Sun

Voyager II (VOY • ih • jer TOO) — a space probe that studied
  Uranus

INDEX

air, 6

atmosphere on Uranus, 35-36

astronomers, 15, 19, 24, 25, 27,
  30, 31, 32, 35-36, 40

Bode, Johann E., 29

clouds on Uranus, 35, 43

comets, 17-18, 23, 44

Copernicus, Nicolaus, 15-16, 18

day on Uranus, 41

Earth, 6, 8, 13-14, 18, 23, 30,
  34, 38

finding Uranus, 20, 22-26

Flamsteed, John, 25, 26

Galileo, 19

Gemini the Twins, 22
gravity, 30
Herschel, Caroline, 21
Herschel, William, 20-21, 22, 23,
    24, 25, 26, 28, 33, 45
Jupiter, 8, 11, 12, 18, 20, 25, 34,
    35, 37, 39, 40, 42
Mars, 8, 11, 12, 18, 25
Mercury, 7, 11, 18, 25
Milky Way, 19-20
moon (of Earth), 12, 30
moons (of other planets), 16-17,
    20
moons (of Uranus), 33-34, 40,
    42
naming Uranus, 27-29
Neptune, 8, 13, 31, 32, 40
ocean on Uranus, 43, 44
orbit, 7, 9, 14, 15, 17, 36
planets, 7-10, 11-14, 15, 16, 17,
    18, 23, 24, 25, 26, 27, 28, 29,
    31, 38

Pluto, 8, 13, 32
rings of Uranus, 37, 43, 44
Saturn, 8, 11, 12, 18, 25, 34, 36-
    37, 39, 40, 42
size of Uranus, 34
sky map, 10
Solar System, 16, 17
space probes, 38, 39, 40, 45
stars, 5-6, 7, 9, 14, 15, 20, 22,
    23, 28
Sun, 5, 7, 9, 11, 14, 16, 17, 23,
    30, 31, 36
Taurus the Bull, 22
telescope, 5, 18, 19, 21, 23, 25,
    33, 34, 38
temperatures on Uranus, 36
Venus, 8, 11, 12, 18, 25
Voyager I, 39
Voyager II, 39, 40, 41, 42
year on Uranus, 36

About the Author

Dennis B. Fradin attended Northwestern University on a partial creative scholarship and was graduated in 1967. His previous books include the Young People's Stories of Our States series for Childrens Press, and Bad Luck Tony for Prentice-Hall. In the True Book series Dennis has written about astronomy, farming, comets, archaeology, movies, space colonies, the space lab, explorers, and pioneers. He is married and the father of three children.